WANT FRIES WITH THAT?

Obesity and the Supersizing of America

Franklin Watts®

A Division of Scholastic Inc.
New York • Toronto • London • Auckland • Sydney
Mexico City • New Delhi • Hong Kong
Danbury, Connecticut

Please note: All information is as up-to-date as possible at the time of publication.

Photographs © 2005: AP/Wide World Photos: 32 (Donna McWilliam), 106 (Lefteris Pitarakis), 45 (Laura Vroman); Corbis Images: 62 (Nick Cunard/eyevine), 108 (Royalty-Free); Getty Images: 87 (William Thomas Cain), 78 (Digital Vision), 76 (David Edwards/National Geographic), 35 (Tim Hall/Photodisc Blue), 103 (Jack Hollingsworth/Photodisc Red), 39 (MedioImages), 3 (Berit Myrekrok/Digital Vision), 27 (Photodisc Collection), 11 (Siede Preis/Photodisc Green), 43 (John A. Rizzo/Photodisc Green), 10 (Stockbyte Gold), 74, 105 (Stockdisc Classic), 33 (Justin Sullivan), 26 (Taxi), 15 (Alex Wong); Photo Researchers, NY: 47 (Antoine Barnaud), 68 (Eye of Science), 71 (Arthur Glauberman), 66 (A. Pasieka), 84 (Alfred Pasieka); PhotoEdit: 30, 31 (Davis Barber), 82 (Mary Kate Denny), 21, 55 (Tony Freeman), 16, 24, 48 (Dennis MacDonald), 54 (Felicia Martinez), 18, 19, 98 (Mark Richards); Phototake: 73 (Carolina Biological Supply Company), 95 (Carol & Mike Werner); PictureQuest: 6, 91 (BananaStock), 4 left, 4 bottom, 5, 8, 9, 12, 14, 17, 34, 36, 37, 52, 56, 57, 59, 60, 85, 89, 92, 101, 115, 119, 121, 128 (Comstock, Inc.), 58 (Thinkstock); Stone/Getty Images/ Josh Mitchell: cover, spot art, 1; The Image Works: 51, 104 (Bob Daemmrich), 93 (EIWA), 25 (Chet Gordon), 100 (Tony Savino), 80 (Michael Siluk), 64 (Topham), 61 (Patrick Watson); Visuals Unlimited: 23 (Dr. Richard Kessel & Dr. Randy Kardon/Tissues & Organs).

Illustration on page 97 by Bob Italiano

Book design by The Design Lab

Library of Congress Cataloging-in-Publication Data
Ingram, Scott.
 Want fries with that? : obesity and the supersizing of America / Scott Ingram.
   p. cm.
 Includes bibliographical references and index.
 ISBN 0-531-16756-9 (alk. paper)
1. Obesity—United States. 2. Convenience foods—Health aspects—United States. 3. Fast-food restaurants—Health aspects—United States. 4. Food habits—United States. I. Title.
RA645.023I54 2006
362.196'398—dc22   2005005619

WANT FRIES WITH THAT?

Obesity and the
Supersizing of America

"French fries are the most often
eaten vegetable in America."
U.S. Office of the Surgeon General, 2003.

by Scott Ingram

CONTENTS

Introduction

Are you hungry? Are you *very, very* hungry? Could you go for a juicy hamburger and a cold drink? Could you go for a couple of burgers, double fries, a milk shake, and cookies? Still not enough? Well, in that case, there's always a Monster Thickburger.

In November 2004, the fast-food chain Hardee's introduced a new choice on its menu: the Monster Thickburger. This is not just the average supersized burger. Instead, the Monster Thickburger is a 2.5-inch-high (6.3-centimeter-high) burger "built" from two ⅓-pound (9-gram) slabs of Angus beef, four strips of bacon, three slices of cheese, and mayonnaise on a buttered sesame seed bun.

Eating one of these monsters means consuming 1,420 **calories** and 107 grams of **fat.** Add some fries and a soda, and that's an additional 900 calories. That would be one meal of more than 2,000 calories—more than the number of calories nutritionists recommend for an entire day for an average adult.

Burgers are delicious, but eating too many of them can be unhealthy.

most recent year for which figures are available for this age group. Some health professionals believe that the situation is probably even worse now. "I think that what we're seeing is that obesity is increasing across the board in adults, adolescents, and children," said Dr. Christopher O'Donnell of the AHA.

Despite the ample evidence that Americans of all ages are overweight, prepackaged snack foods and fast-food outlets provide the meals of choice for many people. In some cases, people choose these foods because they are the only foods available in their communities. In other cases, people eat these foods because their families have traditionally eaten them. In still other cases, young people's food choices are influenced by their peers and by ads on TV and in other media outlets. Health professionals estimate that each year children see about 20,000 snack and fast-food ads on TV alone.[4]

FACTS & STATS

Immigrating to America May Be Dangerous to Your Health!

"Obesity among immigrants may reflect . . . adoption of the U.S. lifestyle, such as increased sedentary behavior and poor dietary patterns."[5] Dr. Mita Sanghavi Goel

The results of a study released in 2004 found that immigrants who come to the United States may be risking their health because of the American way of eating. The lead researcher in the study, Dr. Mita Sanghavi Goel, attributed the rise in obesity rates to two main elements in modern American culture: poor diet and sedentary lifestyles.

The study found that:
- Obesity was rare in immigrants when they first arrived, but not after they lived in the United States for more than 10 years.
- Eight percent of immigrants who had lived in the United States for less than a year were obese. That number jumped to almost 20 percent among immigrants who had lived in the United States for at least 15 years.

This concern about the increasing size of children and adolescents is a recent development. In Carmona's testimony, he stated:

> *Looking back 40 years to the 1960's . . . just over 4 percent of 6- to 17-year-olds were overweight. Since then, that rate has more than tripled, to over 15 percent. And the problem doesn't go away when children grow up. Nearly three out of every four overweight teenagers may become overweight adults.*[2]

Teenagers read scripts at a camp for overweight kids.

The NHANES Study: Boys, Girls, Teens, Tweens

Carmona's comments about teenagers have been verified by a number of studies. For example, the 1999–2002 National Health and Nutrition Examination Survey (NHANES), which measured heights and weights from a representative sample of U.S. residents, showed that more than 15 percent of children and adolescents between the ages of 6 and 19 are overweight and at risk of becoming obese.[3] This classification generally designates people who are at least 20 percent beyond the statistical measure for being over-

Adipose Tissue: Everyone Has It

In most cases, the excess weight that pushes someone from overweight to obese is due to an increase in the amount of fat contained in that person's **adipose tissue.** Adipose tissue gets its name from adipocytes, a group of specialized cells that contain fat. These fat cells, which we all have, are like microscopic bags that contain a drop of fat. The cells are developed during in-

Fat cells are located mainly beneath the skin, where they accumulate and act as protection from heat or insulation from cold.

Fat tends to accumulate in the chest, abdomen, and buttocks of overweight men.

Junk Food in Schools

In late 2004, as news stories about the rise in obesity among young people began to appear frequently in the national press, members of the National Automated Merchandising Society (NAMS) became increasingly concerned about efforts to curb the sale of junk food in schools. In December, the vending machine association recruited Pro Football Hall of Fame player Lynn Swann to lead a campaign against childhood obesity. One aspect of the NAMS campaign was a rating system for the nutritional value of the

Lynn Swann introduces President Bush at a 2003 conference on fitness.

food in vending machines. For example, a red sticker on a candy bar meant that students should eat it infrequently. A green sticker on a healthy snack bar, on the other hand, indicated that it was more nutritious and could be selected more often.

While it's unlikely that vending machines will be removed from all schools, the idea of offering healthy snacks has gained support from students, parents, and vending-machine operators themselves. A 2004 study by the Center for Science in the Public Interest (CSPI) showed that offering healthy food and drinks in vending machines did not reduce profits and in some cases, increased them. In Danbury, Connecticut, for example, a program to place more nutritious foods in vending machines proved successful.

The machines' baked chips, yogurt smoothies, and low-fat popcorn were among the most popular items.

FOR THE RECORD

Billions Spent in U.S. School Vending Machines
Coin-operated snack-dispensing machines are found in many middle schools and high schools. According to industry statistics:
- there are about 7 million vending machines in schools.
- of the $30 billion a year earned from vending machines, more than $4.6 billion is spent in schools.

Schools Fight Back

In some states, the importance of watching one's weight has become part of the school curriculum—and it's more than a topic students read about in books or discuss in health class. For example, in 2004, students in many New Hampshire schools—from kindergarten through twelfth grade—took a new kind of health test for the first time. This wasn't an academic test. Instead, the students had to step on a scale

Snack foods can be healthy if you make smart choices.

in the gym. Volunteers recorded each student's weight and assigned each student an ID number. That way, a student was assured that his or her weight and other health information could only be shared with health professionals and his or her family.[7]

The volunteers then used the student's weight in a mathematical formula to calculate a **body mass index (BMI).** (See "Body Mass Index: What Does It Measure?" below.)

Body Mass Index: What Does It Measure?

Since 2000, doctors and other health specialists have used a new statistic to determine whether a person is underweight, normal, overweight, or obese. This measurement is known as body mass index, or BMI. A person's BMI is a number, usually between 18 and 25, that is calculated by dividing one's weight in pounds by his or her height in inches squared and multiplying by 703. Mathematically, it looks like this:

$$BMI = \frac{\text{weight in pounds}}{\text{height in inches x height in inches}} \times 703$$

For adults, a final number between 18 and 25 is a normal BMI, indicating that a person is within a normal weight range for someone of that height. A man or woman with a BMI over 25 is considered overweight. A person with a BMI over 30 is considered obese.

For children and young adults between 6 and 19 years of age, the BMI reading is interpreted in a different manner. The final calculated number is compared to a chart of other young people of the same age. Separate charts for boys and girls are also used to account for different growth rates and amounts of body fat as boys and girls progress through adolescence. If you calculate your BMI using the formula above (or go to http://www.cdc.gov/nccdphp/dnpa/bmi/calc-bmi.htm to use an online calculator), you can find the percentile for your age on the chart on pages 36–37.

New Hampshire Schools Lead the Way

New Hampshire was the first state to begin a systemwide effort to fight childhood obesity. The state's schools decided to track children's weight when studies showed that the percentage of overweight children in New Hampshire was higher than the national average. According to information collected in 2003, about 18 percent of girls and 22 percent of boys in kindergarten through high school in New Hampshire were overweight or obese, compared to the national average of about 15 percent for both boys and girls.[8]

Junk Food Dumped

In addition to measuring students' BMI, schools across New Hampshire removed junk food from cafeteria vending machines and made efforts to reduce the percentage of fat in cafeteria lunches. Some schools also added a physical fitness test. At Rochester Middle School in New Hampshire, for example, students line up in the gym each fall and spring for their

Exercise is an important part of a healthy lifestyle.

35

What's Your BMI Percentile?

1. Find your age along the horizontal (left-to-right) axis and your BMI along the vertical (up-down) axis.
2. Find your percentile where these two points meet. Your BMI percentile indicates how your measurements compare to other boys or girls in the same age group:

Underweight: Less than the 5th percentile

Ideal weight: Between the 5th and 85th percentiles (50th percentile is average)

Overweight: Between the 85th and 95th percentiles (this means your BMI is higher than 85 percent of boys or girls your age)

Obese: At or above the 95th percentile (your BMI is higher than almost every boy or girl your age)

The American Obesity Association uses the 85th percentile of BMI as a reference point for overweight and the 95th percentile for obesity. According to the AOA, the 95th percentile corresponds to a BMI of 30, which is the marker for obesity in adults. The 85th percentile corresponds to the overweight reference point for adults, which is a BMI of 25.

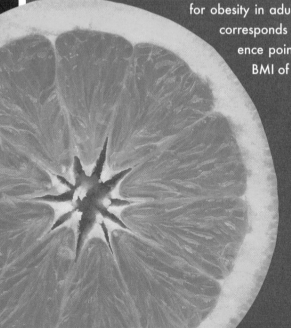

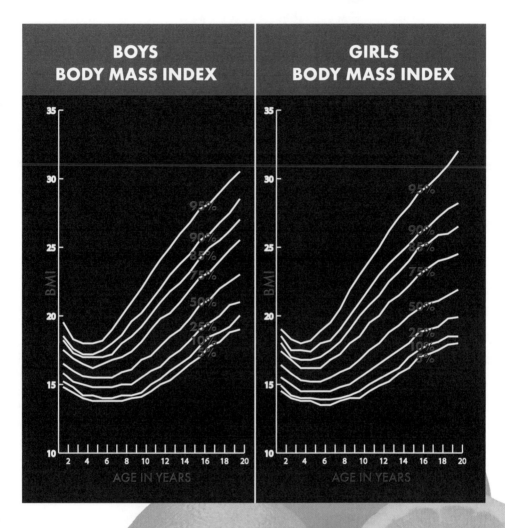

BOYS
BODY MASS INDEX

GIRLS
BODY MASS INDEX

turn at the scale. They also do sit-ups, push-ups, and pull-ups to test their strength, endurance, and flexibility.

Although identification numbers protect students' weights and fitness results, not all students are happy about the required tests. Many feel awkward about the way the tests are conducted. Others are concerned that information about their weight could be spread throughout the school even with their secret ID numbers.

"How Much Do You Weigh?"

"Other kids had to stand 5 feet away from the scale, and sometimes some of the kids have good eyesight where they can actually read the thing," said Sarah Prantis, a sixth-grader at Rochester Middle School. "All the kids were asking: 'How much do you weigh? How much do you weigh?' But I didn't want to tell."

Prantis said the test showed that she was out of shape and that she needed to lose weight. As a result, she took swimming lessons and has joined the school swim team. Now, instead of parking in front of the TV with a bag of chips after school, she walks her three dogs and plays pretend soccer with them.

Rhode Island Follows New Hampshire's Lead

Other states have followed New Hampshire's lead. Rhode Island incorporated the same BMI and fitness test in its schools in 2005. At least 17 states have passed legislation to improve nutrition in school meals. The Massachusetts legislature passed a bill that bans unhealthy food from vending machines in schools. Many school systems have not only cut back on vending machine choices, but also on bake sales and candy sales that were traditional fund-raisers.

California Bans Soda

In 2004, California became the first state to ban soda in its middle schools. In 2003, Texas passed a law that banned the sale of soda, gum, hard candy, and Popsicles during lunch hour or in school cafeterias. Candy bars, potato chips, and french fries, however, were permitted under the law because they contain some nutritional value.

Texas Students Receive "Weight Grades"

Texas schools are also attempting to place the issue of childhood obesity in a place where nobody can miss it: on report cards. In 2005, when studies revealed that one-third of school-age children in Texas were overweight or obese, state senator Leticia Van de Putte proposed a "weight grade" law that would require Texas school districts to include students' BMIs as part of their regular report cards.

Under Van de Putte's law, if the measurement indicated

Drinking too many sugary soft drinks can lead to weight gain.

"We should be just as concerned with students' physical health and performance as we are with their academic performance."
Texas Senator
Leticia Van de Putte

a student was overweight, the school would provide parents with information about links between increased body fat and health problems. "We should be just as concerned with students' physical health and performance as we are with their academic performance," said Van de Putte.

Texas's neighboring state, Arkansas, implemented a similar law during the 2003–2004 school year, when studies revealed similar overweight and obesity statistics among children and adolescents there. In that case, however, the information was sent to parents separately from report cards.

Parents Disapprove

These efforts met with disapproval from educators and parents. Eric Allen, a spokesman for the Association for Texas Professional Educators, said most parents don't need to be told their child is overweight. "It doesn't have a place on a report card," he said. Jean Schultz, a health specialist with the National Middle School Association, warned that schools must be extremely careful when it comes to the issues of weight and students. "Some districts have tried to include a letter home saying, 'Your son or daughter is X number of pounds over the norm,' and parents were offended because they thought the schools were being invasive and unkind to their children."

Among the national organizations that are most supportive of nutrition and weight evaluation programs in schools is the American Obesity Association (AOA). An

AOA reports states, "Outside of the home, children and adolescents spend the majority of their time in school. So, it makes sense that schools provide an environment that promotes healthy nutrition and physical activity habits."[9]

Obesity Report Card for States

In January 2005, the Schaefer Center for Public Policy in Baltimore, Maryland, released a state report card that rates states' efforts to control obesity among children and adolescents. The grading system was based on whether or not the following measures had been introduced or passed into state laws:

- Nutrition standards established for foods sold in schools;
- Vending machines restricted and types of foods monitored;
- Body mass index (BMI) measurements taken in school;
- Recess and physical education required as part of the curriculum;
- Obesity programs and education as part of the health curriculum;
- Obesity research among state government agencies;
- Obesity treatment covered under health care plans;
- Obesity commissions formed by state government.

The report card was not good. No state received an A. The Schaefer gave Ds and Fs to 39 states. The highest grade—B—was given to Arkansas and Connecticut, which both have passed childhood obesity laws.

Obesity Rates for States: Highest to Lowest Prevalence

State	Percent of Obese Adults	Rank	State	Percent of Obese Adults	Rank
Alabama	28.4	1	Kansas	22.6	27
Mississippi	28.1	2	Maryland	21.9	28
West Virginia	27.7	3	Idaho	21.8	29
Indiana	26.0	4	Virginia	21.7	30
Kentucky	25.6	5	Washington	21.7	31
Arkansas	25.2	6	Oregon	21.5	32
Georgia	25.2	7	Nevada	21.2	33
Michigan	25.2	8	New York	20.9	34
Tennessee	25.0	9	Wisconsin	20.9	35
Ohio	24.9	10	Utah	20.8	36
Louisiana	24.8	11	Delaware	20.3	37
Texas	24.6	12	New Hampshire	20.2	38
South Carolina	24.5	13	New Mexico	20.2	39
Oklahoma	24.4	14	Arizona	20.1	40
North Carolina	24.0	15	New Jersey	20.1	41
Washington, DC	24.0	16	Wyoming	20.1	42
Iowa	23.9	17	Florida	19.9	43
Nebraska	23.9	18	Maine	19.9	44
Pennsylvania	23.8	19	Vermont	19.6	45
North Dakota	23.7	20	Connecticut	19.0	46
Missouri	23.6	21	Montana	18.8	47
Alaska	23.5	22	Rhode Island	18.4	48
California	23.2	23	Massachusetts	16.8	49
Illinois	23.2	24	Hawaii	16.4	50
Minnesota	23.0	25	Colorado	16.0	51
South Dakota	22.9	26	**Total average**	**22.8**	

Source: Trust for America's Health

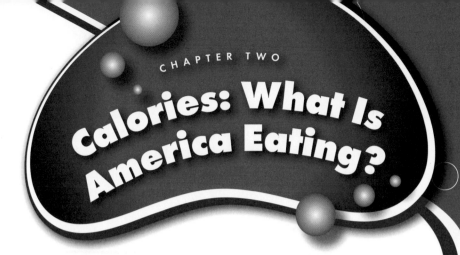

CHAPTER TWO

Calories: What Is America Eating?

Patrick Deuel was always bigger than most kids. In kindergarten, he weighed 90 pounds (41 kg). By the time Deuel was in middle school in his hometown of Valentine, Nebraska, he weighed 250 pounds (113 kg). In some ways, his size was not surprising. He came from a family of large people. Both his father and grandfather weighed more than 300 pounds (136 kg).

That should have been a warning sign, says Deuel now. But as he grew up, he continued to grow "out." In his twenties, Deuel was a restaurant manager and a cook. His job required him to work long hours, and he was free to eat anything he wanted—and as much of it as he could hold. "You'd think you could cook things that would be [healthy]," he said. "But it's a lot more difficult than you think."

Deuel tried many diets over the years, but he never stayed with them. "I'd say just one more day [before a new diet]. It won't hurt me," he recalled. But it soon became easier for him to buy the next-larger size shirt or pants. His career ended in his late twenties when he fell and injured his hip. He was forced to go on medical disability because his weight made walking difficult after the injury.

By the mid-1990s, he had gained so much weight that he refused to go out in public. By 2004, Deuel was too heavy to get out of bed. He was even unable to roll over. Throughout this time, he continued to eat enormous quantities of food. Ironically, he was undernourished because most of the calories he took in came from food that was high in fat and **carbohydrates.**

In June 2004, the 42-year-old Deuel was suffering from shortness of breath, high **blood pressure,** and diabetes. A special van transported him to an obesity clinic at a hospital in Sioux Falls, South Dakota. There, using a special scale used for weighing livestock, doctors determined that the 6-foot-tall (183-cm-tall) Deuel weighed 1,072 pounds (486 kg). He was, in medical terms, morbidly obese, which meant that he would die unless he immediately began to lose weight.

In many cases of morbid obesity, doctors use a surgical procedure to bypass the stomach. But Deuel was too heavy for this procedure, known as **gastric bypass** surgery. Instead, he remained hospitalized—but he began an exercise program and was placed on a 1,200-calorie-a-day diet. By late October, he had lost 420 pounds (191 kg), and the bypass surgery was performed. On January 22, 2005, Deuel was released from the hospital. At that time, he weighed 610 pounds (277 kg). At a check-up in April 2005, Deuel weighed 530 pounds (240 kg). His goal is to get his weight down to 240 pounds (109 kg).

Obviously, Patrick Deuel is an extreme example. Few people have ever topped 1,000 pounds (450 kg). But many of the nutritional habits that resulted in Deuel's morbid obesity can be seen today even in young children, according to doctors across the United States.

Dr. William Cochran, a pediatric gastroenterologist and nutritionist for the Geisinger Clinic in Danville, Pennsylvania, counsels obese adolescents, some of whom weigh between 300 and 400 pounds (135 and 180 kg). An increasing number of the obese kids he counsels, said Cochran, have "adult" obesity-related health problems such as diabetes, high blood pressure, and **liver** disease. Few consider the risks of their dietary habits. "Some kids are drinking a liter or two liters of soda a day," said Cochran. "In 10 to 30 years, the incidence of heart disease and stroke and diabetes are just going to be astronomical."[1]

Patrick Deuel takes a walk with his wife in February 2005.

Weight-Loss Surgery

Some people who are morbidly obese—those with a BMI over 40—choose to lose weight through a type of surgery known as a gastric bypass. Because a gastric bypass is a complicated surgery, it is only used in extreme cases. As a result of this operation:

- **The size of the stomach is reduced.** Surgeons make the patient's stomach smaller by stapling it or wrapping a band around it. This creates a small pouch that allows only a small amount of food to be taken in. The pouch is only slightly larger than a small plastic drinking cup like those that come with cough syrup.
- **Food bypasses areas of the intestines.** After the pouch is formed, a Y-shaped section of the small intestine is attached to it to allow food to bypass the duodenum, which is the first segment of the small intestine, and the jejunum, the second segment of the small intestine.
- **Fewer calories are absorbed in the bloodstream.** Bypassing these areas of the intestines results in a reduction of calories absorbed into the bloodstream.
- **Patients eat smaller portions.** After a bypass, patients must become accustomed to a greatly reduced stomach capacity. Their meals may weigh between 2 and 6 ounces—the size of a deck of cards. A typical dinner, for example, may consist of a slice of chicken, a small scoop of plain mashed potatoes, and a small scoop of peas.
- **The body begins to use calories stored in fat.** The reduction in the size of the patient's stomach results in a sense of fullness after eating small amounts of food. Because of this reduced calorie intake, the body begins to use the calories that had been stored in fat.

Another surgical option for the treatment of obesity is laparoscopic gastric banding. During this procedure, a small incision is made in the patient's abdomen and a gastric band device is placed around the upper part of the stomach to create a small pouch. This reduces the amount of food that a person can eat at one time. One advantage to this procedure is that it doesn't require cutting or stapling of the stomach. In addition, the size of the pouch can be adjusted during a routine outpatient procedure. It is also possible to surgically remove the gastric band if necessary.

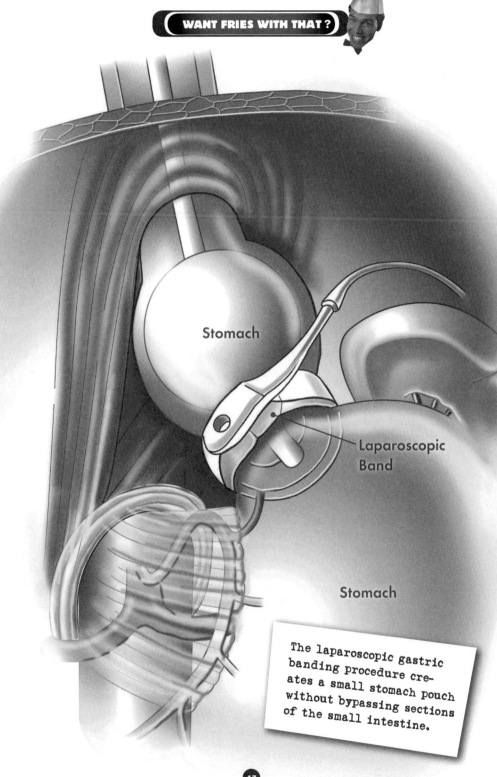

Stomach

Laparoscopic Band

Stomach

The laparoscopic gastric banding procedure creates a small stomach pouch without bypassing sections of the small intestine.

Calories Count!

Young people who drink 1 or 2 liters of soda a day can develop weight-related problems for one main reason: they are consuming more calories than their bodies need. Although the word *calories* is often viewed negatively, in reality, calories are neither good nor bad. Calories are simply a unit of energy. A calorie is defined as the amount of energy, or heat, it takes to raise the temperature of 1 gram of water 1 degree Celsius.

Anything that contains energy contains calories. (Believe it or not, 1 gallon [3.8 liters] of gasoline contains about 31 million calories.) The calories we talk about in food—such as "this piece of bread has 100 calories"—are actually kilocalories, or large calories. In metric measurement, that means 1,000 calories = 1 kilocalorie. One calorie is equal to 4.184 joules, which is a unit of energy that you might someday use in a physics or chemistry class.

A slice of bread containing 100 food calories contains 100,000 regular calories, or 100 kilocalories. To keep things

Nutrition Facts

Serving Size 2 Tbsp. (32g)
Servings Per Container about 35

Amount Per Serving

Calories 190   Calories from Fat 130

	% Daily Value*
Total Fat 16g	25%
Saturated Fat 3g	16%
Cholesterol 0mg	0%
Sodium 150mg	6%
Total Carbohydrate 7g	2%
Dietary Fiber 2g	9%
Sugars 3g	
Protein 8g	

Iron 4%	•	Riboflavin 2%
Niacin 20%	•	Vitamin E 1

Not a significant source

*Percent D.
diet. Your daily
depending on y

Total Fat	
Sat Fat	
Cholesterol	Less
Sodium	Less
Total Carbohydrate	
Dietary Fiber	

Nutrition labels on food packages can help people make better food choices.

48

simple, for the rest of this book we will use the word *calories* instead of *kilocalories*.

Calories: Fuel Your Body Needs

Let's look at an example to get a better idea of what calories mean. The nutritional label on the back of a packet of instant maple-and-brown-sugar oatmeal states that a single packet—that is, one serving—has 120 calories. Scientifically speaking, if we poured this packet of oatmeal into a dish, set it on fire, and burned it completely, enough energy would be produced to raise the temperature of 120 kilograms of water by 1 degree Celsius.

> Just as cars need gas to operate, humans need energy in order to "run."

Of course oatmeal is for eating, not for science experiments. A person who ate this oatmeal would "burn" the calories through a process called **metabolism.** Metabolism occurs when food is broken down into molecules in the digestive tract and sent through the bloodstream to the cells. There they are either absorbed and used immediately or stored for future use. Remember the body's storehouse, adipose cells? Any calories from the oatmeal that are not used immediately would end up there.

A Measure of Energy

No matter how they are counted, calories are a measure of energy. Just as cars need gas to operate, humans need energy in order to "run." We use energy when we breathe, move, and think. We also use energy that we may not even be aware of, such as the energy our bodies use to digest the food we eat. All of this energy comes from food. The number of calories contained in a certain item of food is simply a numeric statement about how much usable energy the food contains.

A person who eats exactly the number of calories that he or she burns will maintain a constant weight. A person who takes in more calories than she burns will gain weight. A person who burns more calories than he eats will lose weight. So, in one sense, a calorie of protein is no different from a calorie of carbohydrates or a calorie of fat.

It's important to understand, however, that equal amounts of carbohydrates, protein, and fats do not contain the same number of calories. One gram (0.035 ounce) of carbohydrates has 4 calories. One gram of protein has 4 calories. One gram of fat has 9 calories. Can you see how a person who eats high-fat foods can eat the same amount (in grams) as a person who eats protein or carbohydrates but actually consume more calories?

How Many Calories Do You Need?

Most nutritionists agree that the average adult needs about 2,000 calories a day to keep his or her body running efficiently. (Remember, there are 1,420 calories in a single Monster Thickburger!) Your body, however, might need more than 2,000 calories depending on your age, gender, and the amount of physical activity you get. Doctors estimate that boys between the ages of 7 and 10 need about

2,000 calories per day; boys between the ages of 11 and 14 need about 2,500 calories a day; and boys 15 to 18 years old who are active and developing need approximately 3,000 calories a day. Girls between 7 and 10 need about 2,000 calories a day, while adolescent girls between 11 and 18 need about 2,200 calories a day. Physically active girls need between 2,800 and 3,000 calories per day. There are three things that determine the number of calories any given person needs to consume in a day:

People who are physically active need more calories than people who are not active to meet their daily energy requirements.

1. Your BMR: The Amount of Energy Your Body Needs To Function

Basal metabolic rate (BMR) is the amount of energy the body needs to keep the heart beating, the lungs breathing, the kidneys functioning, and the body temperature steady. These activities, which few of us ever think about, burn between 60 and 70 percent of our daily calories. In general, because boys are physically larger and more active than girls, they have a higher BMR—which is one reason they have a higher recommended calorie intake.

2. Physical Activity: The Number of Calories You Burn

Physical activity also plays an important role in determining caloric needs. But physical activity isn't just playing basketball or snowboarding. Any movement you make, from brushing your teeth to bending over to tie your shoes, burns calories. One interesting fact about physical activity is that your body continues to burn calories after you are at rest. That's why exercise is an ingredient in any weight-loss plan, even if, like Deuel, you begin by taking just a few steps a day.

3. The Thermic Effect of Food: The Amount of Energy Your Body Uses to Digest Food

The final category that determines the total number of calories needed per day is the **thermic effect** of food. This term refers to the amount of energy your body uses to digest the food you eat. In other words, you need to burn calories to break down the food you take into your body. In most cases, this process amounts to about 10 percent of the calories we eat in a day.

When You Take in More Calories Than Your Body Burns

Looking at the case of Patrick Deuel in relation to these three requirements, it's apparent why his body began to fail as he grew heavier. He became so large that his heart had to work extra hard to pump blood to all parts of his body. His lungs had to work extra hard to take in enough air to supply oxygen to his blood as his heart pumped. And his kidneys and intestines had to work extra hard to excrete the waste products that resulted from his huge intake of food.

This meant that his BMR was extremely high—the more he ate, the more he needed to eat.

Deuel's high calorie intake, in turn, required large amounts of calories to digest his food—the thermic effect. As a result, Deuel had fewer calories available to fuel his physical activity. Ironically, because he was so heavy, he required many more calories than a normal person would even to roll over.

Of course, very few people ever reach the level of morbid obesity that Deuel reached. But what happens if you take in more calories than your body burns? Simple—it is stored as fat. This is how the body saves energy for a time when it is needed. Health experts have determined that 3,500 extra calories—those that are not used in any of the three ways—will be stored in the body as 1 pound (0.45 kg) of fat. Using the opposite example, anyone who burns 3,500 more calories than she eats—through exercising or reducing food intake—will use 1 pound of stored fat for energy.

FACTS & STATS

How Do We Know We're Hungry?

Our stomachs may growl or we may feel dizzy. But actually, it's all in our heads! The control system that tells you it's time to eat is located in your brain. The urge to eat comes from an area in the brain called the **hypothalamus**. Scientists do not know exactly how the hypothalamus understands that the body needs to eat, but they have studied cases in which people who have suffered damage to one part of the hypothalamus will overeat with no control. Damage to a different part of the hypothalamus may cause a person to have no appetite at all. Scientists now believe that a balance between these two areas sends a signal to the rest of the body that it's time to eat. Scientists also have learned that the hypothalamus is the area of the brain that controls body temperature and feelings such as anger and pleasure.

All Calories are NOT Created Equal

While it is true that calories are a measure of energy, not all calories are created equal. The type of calories one takes in depends on the type of food one eats. What are some of the foods you have eaten today? Did you have toast or cereal for breakfast? Did you drink milk or soda? Did you have a ham sandwich and an apple or some peanuts for lunch? All of these foods—and almost anything else you have eaten—contain seven basic parts: carbohydrates, proteins, fats, vitamins, minerals, fiber, and water. Of these seven, the three main building blocks—the calorie containers—are carbohydrates, protein, and fat.

Does it matter how many calories we eat from each source? Definitely. Foods containing carbohydrates and proteins provide healthier calorie containers than foods high in fats. This doesn't mean that we should not eat any fat. Fat is what allows the body to absorb the vitamins in our food. But we only need a little bit of fat to do this job.

According to the U.S. Food and Drug Administration (FDA), no more than 30 percent of a person's daily calories should come from fat. Using the 2,000 calories-per-day measure, that equals no more than 600 calories—or 67 grams—of fat per day.[2] In 2004, doctors and nutritionists who

Meat, fish, eggs, cheese, and nuts are all good sources of protein.

specialize in obesity-related issues said that fat calories should comprise only 25 percent of a person's daily intake. That's 56 grams of fat per day for a 2,000-calorie diet. (The Monster Thickburger has 107 grams of fat!)

Calories from Carbohydrates

In order to understand why calorie containers are important, let's look at each one individually. Carbohydrates provide your body with its basic fuel. Your body uses the calories in carbohydrates the way a car engine uses gasoline. Just as gasoline is a by-product of oil, **glucose** is the by-product of carbohydrates that fuel your body. Glucose is commonly known as blood sugar. Cells take glucose from the blood and change it into energy to "drive" your cells.

Because glucose is a sugar, it tastes sweet. Some foods contain sugars besides glucose. You may have heard of fructose, the main sugar in fruits; lactose, a sugar found in milk; and sucrose, also known as white sugar or table sugar.

Bread, rice, pasta, and cereal are foods that are high in carbohydrates.

Glucose and fructose are carbohydrates that are absorbed directly into the bloodstream through the intestines. Lactose and sucrose must be changed into glucose in the digestive tract before they can be absorbed into the blood. In either case, these carbohydrate sugars enter the bloodstream relatively quickly.

Many people connect the term *carbohydrates* with foods such as bread and spaghetti. In nutritional terms, these foods are called complex carbohydrates, but we generally call them starches. In a way, starches are one step away from the carbohydrates in fructose and sucrose. That's because starches are like plant storehouses. Grains such as wheat, corn, oats, and rice, and vegetables such as potatoes and plantains, are high in starch and store energy as they grow. Once they are harvested and eaten as food, it's the job of our digestive system to break down the starch into glucose so it can enter the bloodstream.

It takes the body longer to break down a starch than it does to absorb glucose. For example, drinking a can of soda sweetened with sugar will put glucose into the bloodstream at about 30 calories a minute. The complex carbohydrates

HEALTHY CHOICES

What's for Breakfast?

Nutritionists generally agree that breakfast is the most important meal we eat because it provides energy for the day ahead. So, if you're sleepy and you're looking for quick energy before school, is it better to have a candy bar or cereal for breakfast? Both put glucose into your bloodstream, but one is better for you than the other.

Cereal is a better choice. Why? One reason is that the carbohydrates in cereal are released slowly and steadily into your bloodstream over a longer period of time. You have a steady supply of energy. A chocolate bar, on the other hand, releases glucose into your bloodstream almost immediately—which is not necessarily a good thing.

in potatoes, which are digested more slowly, allow glucose to enter the bloodstream at a rate of 2 calories per minute. Athletes such as distance runners and long-distance bicycle riders often eat large quantities of starch before events so that glucose will be pumped steadily into their bloodstream as they race.

Calories from Protein

If carbohydrates are the "gas" that makes a body run, protein is its steel framework—the muscles that move our bodies. Protein is made up of molecules called **amino acids.** These acids are the building blocks of our cells. There are two types of amino acids: essential and nonessential. Nonessential amino acids are acids that your body can create out of other chemicals found in your body. Essential amino acids cannot be created, and therefore the only way to get them is through food.

Animal and Vegetable Proteins

The protein that provides amino acids in our diets is found in foods from both animals and vegetables. Animal sources—meat, milk, and eggs—give humans what is known as complete protein, meaning that they contain all of the essential amino acids. Vegetable foods usually lack certain essential amino acids. For example, rice is low in two essential amino acids. Beans, however, contain the two acids that rice lacks. Eating a dish of rice and beans will provide complete protein. Nuts, beans, and soybeans contain almost all of the essential amino acids. Once the protein-containing food is in the body, the digestive system breaks it down into separate amino acids that then enter the bloodstream. Cells then use the amino acids as building blocks to create muscle tissue.

Just as the body requires carbohydrates, it must also take in protein. The U.S. government's recommended daily allowance (RDA) for protein is 0.36 gram of protein per pound of body weight. That means that a 100-pound (45 kg) person needs 36 grams of protein per day. How much protein is that? Take a look.

The label on a jar of peanut butter states that one serving—2 tablespoons—contains 7 grams of protein. A slice of bread has 2 grams of protein, and a glass of milk contains about 8 grams of protein. So, a 100-pound person who has a peanut-butter sandwich and a glass of milk for lunch will consume 19 grams of protein, more than half of his or her RDA.

Calories from Fat

Foods that contain fat are essential to our health, but consuming large quantities of fat-containing foods can lead to severe health problems. Like carbohydrates and protein, fats appear in various types of food. Meat such as beef contains fat. So does the skin of chicken. Fish has fat too. Bread and pastries, such as muffins,

French fries and other fried foods should be eaten in moderation.

are made with vegetable oils, shortening, or lard—all fats. Fried foods, such as french fries, are cooked in heated oils.

All Fats Are Greasy and Smooth

The one thing that all fats have in common is that they are greasy and smooth. Nutritionists separate fats into two categories: saturated and unsaturated. Saturated fats are normally solid at room temperature, while un-saturated fats remain liquid at room tem-perature. Vegetable oil, such as olive oil, is one common source of unsatu-rated fat. Butter, margarine, and the whitish fat in raw steak are examples of saturated fats.

When we eat foods containing fat, our digestive systems break the fat down into chemicals called triglycerides—in much the same way that carbohydrates are broken down into glucose. The triglyc-erides are carried in the bloodstream to muscle cells—for fuel—or to adipose cells for storage.

Fat: An Important Daily Requirement

Fat is an important part of the body's daily calorie intake. It acts as a transportation system to carry the vitamins from foods into the body. In the same way that protein supplies the body with essential amino acids, fat supplies the body with essential fatty acids. The body cannot make its own fatty acids. They can only be found in foods.

Fat is also a good source of energy because it contains twice as many calories per gram as do carbohydrates or proteins. Your body can burn fat as fuel when necessary. The U.S. government, however, recommends that no more than 30 percent of your daily calories come from fat.

Is All Fat the Same?

Some types of fat are more harmful to a person's health than other types. The most harmful fats are saturated fat and trans fat. Both of these fats can increase a person's risk of heart disease. Experts believe that trans fat may carry an even greater health risk than saturated fat.

Saturated and Trans Fat

Saturated and trans fats come mostly from animal products. Some tropical oils, such as palm kernel oil and coconut oil, also contain saturated fat. Trans fat is found in dairy and meat products, but one of the most common sources of trans fat is hydrogenated vegetable oil. Hydrogenated oils are liquids that have been changed into a solid form of fat and combined with hydrogen to prevent them from losing their flavor or spoiling. Trans fats are often found in packaged goods, like cookies, crackers, and potato chips, which can remain on grocery-store shelves without spoiling. Trans fats are also found in fried foods such as french fries and doughnuts. Because saturated fat and trans fat are tied to heart disease, a gram of one of these fats is worse for a person's health than a gram of unsaturated fat.

Packaged foods, such as muffins, cookies, and chips often contain unhealthy trans fats.

Unsaturated Fats

Unsaturated fats are divided into polyunsaturated and monounsaturated fats. Polyunsaturated fat is found in soybean, corn, sesame, and sunflower oils, or fish and fish oil. Monounsaturated fat is found in olives, olive or canola oil, most nuts and their oils, and avocados. These foods are the best sources of fat for a balanced diet.

A New Life for Patrick Deuel

As news of Patrick Deuel's success spread, he received more than 2,000 letters of support from around the world. A group of 75 middle school students in Chicago, Illinois, sent so many letters that Deuel called the school to thank the kids.

In late January 2005, Deuel left Avera-McKennan Hospital in Sioux Falls, South Dakota. Seven months after he checked in because he was near death from obesity-related problems, he had lost almost 500 pounds (225 kg). He arrived at the hospital in a special ambulance with a high-power lift to move him. He left the hospital by walking to a sport utility vehicle driven by his wife, Edith. On Valentine's Day he was able to take a short walk outside of his home with Edith. Deuel plans to become a motivational speaker and talk about his battles with weight. His goal is to get his weight down to 240 pounds (109 kg). The last time he weighed that much, he was in sixth grade.

Olive, corn, and safflower oil are low in saturated fat.

CHAPTER THREE

Obesity's Effects on Mind and Body

Morgan Spurlock was sick, and his doctors were worried. He had gained 17 pounds (7.7 kg) in 20 days. He had headaches, breathing problems, and chest pains. His liver was overflowing with fat. He was depressed and tired all the time. Spurlock, who had once been a healthy 6-foot-2-inch-tall (188-cm-tall), 185-pound (84 kg) man, had begun to show rapid signs of health-related obesity problems. All of this had occurred because the number of calories he ate per day had doubled, and he had avoided all exercise. Why had Spurlock done this to himself? Because he wanted to make a movie.

In 2004, Spurlock filmed a documentary titled *Super Size Me: A Film of Epic Proportions,* which became one of the most successful films of the year

Director Morgan Spurlock poses outside a McDonald's restaurant in London, England.

and earned an Oscar nomination for Best Documentary. He had originally come up with the idea for it in 2002, when he saw a news report about two teenage girls whose parents had sued McDonald's, blaming the fast-food company for their daughters' obesity-related problems.

Spurlock objected to the suit. He felt that personal responsibility was as much a factor in this case as food choice. But he also became curious about the enormous presence of fast food in American society when he learned that there were eighty-three McDonald's restaurants in Manhattan, New York, where he lived. This led him to develop his project: a documentary movie about his experience of eating nothing but McDonald's food for thirty days in a row—breakfast, lunch, and dinner. He chose McDonald's simply because it was the world's largest fast-food chain. At the time, its outlets accounted for 43 percent of all fast food served in the United States.

The Supersizing of Spurlock

Spurlock set certain rules for filming his experiment. He would only eat what was available off the menu, including water. He would not take any vitamins or other health supplements. He would not "supersize" any item unless asked—then he would agree to the larger portion. He had to eat every item on the McDonald's menu at least once.

In order to make his experiment more realistic, Spurlock also decided to give up his normal daily running. That would make his experience more closely resemble that of the 60 percent of Americans who get little or no exercise. His only exertion would be setting up cameras and walking into and out of McDonald's outlets across the United States—in all, fewer than 2,500 steps per day.

Before he began filming, Spurlock was examined by

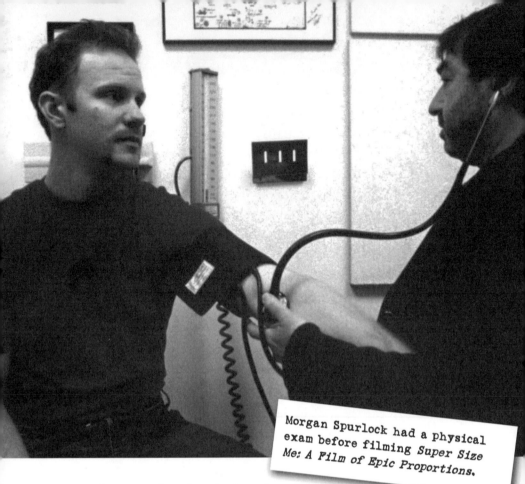

Morgan Spurlock had a physical exam before filming Super Size Me: A Film of Epic Proportions.

doctors who found that his blood pressure was normal and his BMI was 23.8—within the normal range for his height and weight. Doctors estimated that because he was a relatively large man who exercised regularly, his normal daily intake should be about 2,500 calories. On the first day of filming, he had eaten that many calories by the time he finished lunch.

Ten Pounds in One Week

After the first week, Spurlock had gained 10 pounds (4.5 kg). Since it takes 3,500 calories over one's daily intake to add 1 pound (0.45 kg) of fat, Spurlock was taking in at least 6,000 calories per day. Divided by three meals, that means he was eating 2,000 calories per meal—the average recommended daily intake for a young adult. In addition to calories, the food he ate resulted in his taking in about 1 pound (0.45 kg) of sugar and 0.25 pound (0.11 kg) of fat per day.

It was expected that Spurlock would gain weight. What worried doctors by the second week was that Spurlock had eaten so much fat that his adipose cells could not process it, and it had begun to accumulate in his liver. The liver is one of the body's most vital organs because it removes toxins from the bloodstream. Spurlock was approaching the point of liver failure, and doctors advised him to end the filming ten days early.

25 Pounds Later and Emotionally "Horrible"

In the end, however, Spurlock completed the 30-day experiment—and gained about 25 pounds (11 kg). For Spurlock, however, gaining weight wasn't the worst side effect of his experiment. As he put it, he felt "horrible [both] physically [and] emotionally. I was ashen, pale, my energy level was low. Then I'd eat the food, I'd feel great, and an hour later I'd feel hungry again."[1]

Of course, Spurlock's experiment was so extreme that it exceeded the eating patterns of many obese people. He ate more fast food in a month than nutritionists recommend over a period of five years. Guy Russo, president of McDonald's, pointed out this fact when questioned by reporters, calling Spurlock's experiment "stupid." "No one eats McDonald's food three times a day, every day, and no one should," said Russo. "We believe, and have always believed, that McDonald's can be eaten as part of a well-balanced diet. What Spurlock set out to do, which was double his daily calorie intake, deliberately not exercise and overeat, was totally irresponsible."[2]

Obesity and Heart Disease

Like Spurlock, people who consume large quantities of calories, fat, sugar, and carbohydrates—over a period of years rather than weeks—are putting their lives at risk. One of the greatest risks faced by overweight and obese people is heart disease.

Increased Cholesterol Levels

The heart is the most important muscle in the body, and it needs a constant supply of oxygen-filled blood in order to function. Blood is carried in and out of the heart by a complex network of arteries and veins that web its surface. If an artery becomes narrowed or blocked, the blood supply will be diminished or cut off. This narrowing or blockage of the arteries is usually caused by an accumulation of a waxlike fat called cholesterol. Although the body manufactures and controls most of its cholesterol naturally, the substance is also found in fatty foods—and that is how obese people put themselves at risk. People who are obese generally have high cholesterol levels in their blood.

Disease of the Arteries

When blood vessels—arteries, veins, and capillaries—are narrowed by cholesterol build-

The heart has to work harder to pump blood through vessels clogged with cholesterol.

up, a condition called **atherosclerosis** results. This condition forces the heart to work harder than normal to pump blood through the obstructed vessels. This problem occurs among people with a normal BMI who are smokers or have hereditary heart disease. People who are overweight or obese, however, not only risk atherosclerosis, but also must take in higher than normal quantities of oxygen because their hearts have to work harder to pump blood to the excess fat around the body. That is why it is not unusual for an obese person to use an oxygen tank to supply the extra oxygen needed.

High Blood Pressure

Over a period of time, this extra energy requirement, coupled with narrowed arteries, can cause the heart to become enlarged, which in turn results in high blood pressure. This condition is a leading cause of heart attacks or strokes.

High blood pressure can also have a harmful effect on the kidneys. The kidneys are two bean-shaped organs located on each side of the spine. They clean the blood, and the waste they remove is excreted in the urine through a complicated system of filtering tubes. In order to remove waste, all of the blood in the body passes through the kidneys approximately twenty times an hour. People who are obese and who have high blood pressure risk stressing their kidneys to the point that they fail.

Obesity and Cancer

In January 2005, the American Cancer Society released the results of a study that tracked the causes of death for Americans in 2002. For the first time, according to the study, cancer surpassed heart disease as the number-one killer

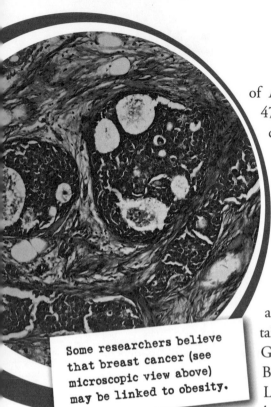

Some researchers believe that breast cancer (see microscopic view above) may be linked to obesity.

of Americans. In 2002, about 476,000 Americans died of cancer. And according to Dr. Harmon Eyre, the Cancer Society's longtime chief medical officer, one-third of those cancer deaths were related to obesity.

Recent studies like this one have revealed a relationship between excess body fat and the risk of developing certain types of cancer. In 2002, Dr. George Bray of the Pennington Biomedical Research Center in Louisiana discussed the studies he conducted for the American Institute of Cancer Research (AICR) on the connection between obesity and cancer. "The more we understand about obesity, the more we realize that . . . being overweight and inactive . . . makes it easier for cancer to gain a foothold," said Bray.

Bray pointed out that most people regard body fat simply as excess skin that accumulates in specific places such as the belly, waist, back, and arms. In addition, explained Bray, people think of fat as merely a "storehouse" of energy that can be called upon for extra energy when needed. "We imagine . . . extra pounds just sit there quietly, storing energy, until we 'burn' them," Bray said.[3]

Increased Hormones Released by Fat Cells

Bray's research indicated that fat tissue is not "quiet." Instead, fat cells constantly produce hormones and substances that are secreted into the bloodstream. These natural chemicals, Bray's research indicated, trigger reactions in other cells throughout the body. It is this process that appears to create the conditions for certain cancerous cells to develop.

The chemicals secreted by fat cells are normal elements found in the body, such as sex hormones and other components of a person's basic body chemistry. In a person of normal weight, the secretion of these elements spurs cells to grow in a controlled manner. But Bray and other scientists now believe that the excess body fat in an obese person causes above-average amounts of chemicals to be released into the bloodstream. The result is that an obese person's cells are triggered to grow and to divide at an increasingly rapid rate.

It is this overly rapid cell division that raises the cancer risk, Bray claimed. The more often cells divide and replicate, the greater the chance that a cell will mutate, or change its structure. This, in turn, increases the likelihood that a cell will mutate into a cancer cell.

Excess Body Fat Linked to Some Cancers

The increased chemical activity in fat cells carries another risk. In all animals, including humans, body fat is the location where carcinogens, cancer-causing chemicals, settle. Thus, in women, excess body fat has been linked to a higher rate of breast and uterine cancer. Obese men are at higher risk of developing cancer of the colon and the prostate gland.

The strongest evidence for a connection between body fat and cancer is in the frequency of breast cancer for women over 50, according to Bray. Studies on overweight and obese women in this age group show higher levels of the female hormone estrogen than is found among women over 50 whose weight is normal. Bray and other specialists believe these high hormone levels indicate a strong cancer risk because the fat cells are actively releasing estrogen into the bloodstream. This extra estrogen has been clearly linked to breast cancer.

For Bray and other researchers, the body fat–breast cancer connection may be only one of many such links. Some cancer specialists believe that excess body fat will eventually be tied to cancer of the breast, ovary, abdomen, and prostate.

Cancer Risks Can Increase as Body Weight Increases
Scientists now say that while obesity is thought to raise cancer risk significantly, even people who are overweight face extra cancer risk. Bray reviewed several studies that have linked obesity to certain types of cancers and to cancer in general. In other words, he said, cancer risk increases as body weight increases. In fact, the American Institute for Cancer Research estimates that obesity is associated with more than 25 percent of all cases of breast cancer, colon cancer, kidney cancer, and esophageal (throat) cancer.

"There are likely many factors that explain why obesity and overweight increase cancer risk," said Bray, "[but] we're seeing the same bottom line over and over again: avoiding weight gain is one of the most important things we can do to prevent cancer."[4]

Obesity's Effect on Internal Organs

While cancer can take years to develop, the intake of high-fat foods in large amounts can have a more immediate impact on other internal organs. This was one of the more

alarming side effects of Spurlock's experiment. His doctors were most concerned about the elevated fat level in his liver. Within twenty days, they said, his liver resembled the liver of a person who had a serious alcohol-abuse problem. One doctor was so concerned that he insisted Spurlock stop his project because he could do permanent harm to his liver.

Liver Damage

Luckily for Spurlock, his decision to continue filming has resulted in no permanent damage to his liver. Many people who are overweight and obese, however, risk harming not only their livers but also other internal organs such as the **gallbladder** and the kidneys.

Of these organs, the liver is the most critical to our survival. It is a large organ—about 3 pounds (1.4 kg) in an adult—and each day it carries out hundreds of functions that keep us healthy. One of these responsibilities is to produce a chemical called bile, which helps to break down fats so they can be absorbed in the blood. The liver stores fats,

Three human liver samples show the difference between a normal liver (left), a fatty liver (middle), and the liver of a person with cirrhosis (right).

a form of sugar called **glycogen,** iron, and vitamins for use when the body needs them. It also receives blood from the stomach and intestines and cleanses it of waste matter and harmful substances, such as drugs and alcohol, that enter the body. Fatty liver, the condition that Spurlock developed, is just what it sounds like—a buildup of fat in the liver cells. In most cases, fat builds up in the liver due to alcohol abuse, extreme weight gain, or diabetes.

As serious as fatty liver is, doctors consider it a warning sign. That's why Spurlock's doctors were concerned. Left untreated, a fatty liver can swell and begin to form scar tissue. Known as cirrhosis of the liver, this condition is usually associated with severe alcoholism. Today, nonalcoholic fatty liver disease is so widespread that researchers believe 25 percent of the population shows signs of this type of liver damage.

Gallstones and Pancreatitis

The internal organ most closely connected to the liver is the gallbladder. This small, pear-shaped storage sac is located on the right side of the abdomen beneath the liver. Its main function is to store bile from the liver. When food is digested, the gallbladder releases bile into the small intestine, where it helps dissolve fats and remove cholesterol and waste from the body.

People who are overweight or obese are at risk of developing a condition known as **gallstones,** which are hard particles of cholesterol. Gallstones are formed when a person eats foods high in carbohydrates, fats, and sugar that flood the liver with an oversupply of cholesterol. The overflow crystallizes into gallstones.

A gallstone attack usually begins as a steady stabbing pain in the upper abdomen. Attacks may last only twenty or thirty minutes, but more often they last several hours. Gallstones may also block the flow of digestive chemicals secreted from another small organ, the **pancreas,** into the small intestine. This leads to pancreatitis, an inflammation of the pancreas, which is another condition that can result from alcohol abuse.

Research shows that Native Americans have a genetic tendency to secrete high levels of cholesterol, and, as a result, they have the highest rate of gallstones of any ethnic group in the United States.

Excess cholesterol can lead to the formation of gallstones.

FACTS & STATS

Pancreatitis

Your pancreas is located on the left side of your abdomen, behind the stomach, and above the upper section of the small intestine.

- Its job is to produce digestive chemicals called enzymes which break down food and chemicals called hormones that regulate blood glucose. When gallstones block the flow of digestive enzymes, the pancreas begins to digest itself. This causes the inflammation known as pancreatitis.
- In the most serious cases, enzymes and waste products may leak into the bloodstream and damage the heart, lungs, and kidneys. In some cases, this causes death.

Obesity and Type 2 Diabetes

While fatty liver and gallstones are serious indicators of health problems and disease, doctors and other health professionals agree that one of the most alarming effects of the obesity crisis in the United States is the rapid rise in type 2 diabetes. Diabetes is a disease that results from an imbalance between the amount of glucose in the blood and a hormone called **insulin.** Remember, glucose is a form of sugar that is the body's main source of energy. When you eat, glucose is absorbed from the intestines and carried through the bloodstream to all of the body's cells. Because your body is constantly "running," whether you are active or not, it needs a steady supply of glucose.

If you only eat three times per day, the food you take in cannot constantly supply the energy you need. To maintain a constant supply, your body turns to the pancreas for two hormones: glucagon and insulin. The job of keeping glucose levels steady between meals falls to glucagon. When the glucose level falls, glucagon signals cells to release glucose from the fat cells and liver where it is stored.

Insulin is required every time we eat anything, from a candy bar to a meal. When our intestines take nutrients from the food, this digestive process alerts the pancreas to release insulin into the blood, where it enables cells to absorb glucose, fatty acids, and amino acids. Insulin also acts as a regulator to prevent

People with diabetes need to regularly monitor their blood sugar levels.

too much glucose from remaining in the bloodstream. And that's where diabetes comes in.

Risk: Type 2 Diabetes

There are two types of diabetes. Type 1, which is also called juvenile diabetes or insulin-dependent diabetes, results from the body's inability to produce insulin. This type of diabetes is found in 5 to 10 percent of cases, and in most cases it is inherited.

The other form of diabetes, type 2, is usually discovered after age 30, which is why it is sometimes called adult onset diabetes. With type 2 diabetes, the body makes too much insulin in an effort to keep glucose levels normal. Eventually, this overproduction causes the body to lose its ability to produce enough insulin to keep glucose levels normal, which results in high blood sugar levels. Doctors are uncertain what causes this to occur, but they do know that excess blood sugar is stored in the liver and adipose cells. They theorize that when these cells become full, they cannot take in more blood sugar, and over time the whole system for balancing glucose in the bloodstream breaks down.

Although doctors do not know what triggers this imbalance, research has established that people who are overweight or obese have a high risk of developing type 2 diabetes. What makes this form of diabetes particularly dangerous is that it can take several years before it is detected; in adults it is usually not detected until middle age. The two main symptoms that occur are increased thirst and frequent urination. These symptoms arise because extra glucose circulating in the body absorbs water from the tissues and dehydrates them. In response, people drink a lot of fluids, which leads to more frequent urination.

Blindness, Numbness, and Slow-Healing Wounds

By the time people are aware of these symptoms, however, damage may already have occurred. The loss of water causes the blood to thicken, which slows circulation. Slow blood circulation causes numbness in the hands and feet, decreased vision, slow-healing wounds, and frequent infections. Eventually, type 2 diabetes can cause blindness and kidney failure, as well as leg and foot amputations. More than 200,000 people die each year of diabetes-related complications.

About 90 percent of people with type 2 diabetes are overweight or obese. The increase in cases of type 2 diabetes in children and adolescents since 1990 is even more disturbing to doctors and health professionals. While only 3 percent of all childhood diabetics had type 2 diabetes before 1992, it had risen rapidly to 16 percent of cases by 2000. People affected with type 2 diabetes belong to all ethnic groups, but it is more common in non-white groups. American Indian youth have the

Young American Indians have a high rate of type 2 diabetes.

highest prevalence of this form of diabetes. It is also found in high rates among African American children and Hispanic children, especially those of Mexican descent.

"Super-Sized" DVDs Available For Schools

In March 2005, Spurlock released a specially edited DVD of *Super Size Me* for use in schools with students in grades 6 through 12. In addition to segments of the original film, the DVD contained interviews with nutritionists and doctors. Spurlock worked with private foundations to raise money so that the DVD could be supplied free to low-income school districts. His decision to create a DVD for schools arose from his concern about cuts to gym classes and reduced health education in schools, as well as his travels to school lunchrooms around the country. "We're educating kids in the classroom, but we're abandoning them in the lunchroom," Spurlock said. "Schools are the perfect place to teach nutrition."

Obesity and Metabolic Syndrome

While Spurlock's experience did not last long enough for diabetes to develop, his doctors became concerned about his health because several serious health risks arose almost simultaneously: fatty liver, high blood pressure, weight gain, and high cholesterol. In combination, these symptoms could have become life threatening if Spurlock had continued his experiment beyond 30 days.

A Combination of Warning Signs

A short time after *Super Size Me* was nominated for an Academy Award in early 2005, the symptoms that Spurlock developed were reported in the *Washington Post* as **metabolic syndrome.** Researchers at Harvard University Medi-

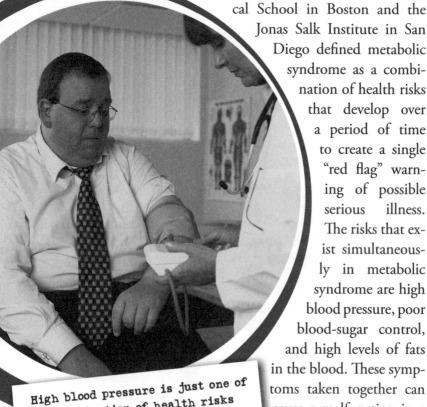

cal School in Boston and the Jonas Salk Institute in San Diego defined metabolic syndrome as a combination of health risks that develop over a period of time to create a single "red flag" warning of possible serious illness. The risks that exist simultaneously in metabolic syndrome are high blood pressure, poor blood-sugar control, and high levels of fats in the blood. These symptoms taken together can cause a malfunction in a person's metabolism—the process by which food is broken down into molecules and carried to the cells in the bloodstream.

High blood pressure is just one of the combination of health risks known as metabolic syndrome.

Many Americans Go Undiagnosed

Most people with metabolic syndrome do not realize they are at risk. The Howard–Salk report warns that unless steps are taken to identify people with the syndrome, there is a strong possibility of dramatic increases in heart attacks, strokes, diabetes, liver disease, and certain types of cancer as the obesity rate rises in the United States.

According to the report, at least 64 million Americans—about one-third of adults over age 20—may have the syndrome, which includes about 50 percent of elderly Americans. Mexican Americans and African American women are among the highest risk groups for the syndrome. It has also been identified in an increasing number of overweight children.

Despite extensive research, scientists remain uncertain exactly how weight gain can cause a person's metabolism to break down. Most now disagree with the former theory of the fat cell as little more than a storage area for energy. It is now believed that fat cells release chemical signals in the form of hormones that affect the body. The accumulation of fat in the abdomen and the liver appears to be especially dangerous, according to research. "At some point fat becomes toxic," said Ronald M. Evans of the Salk Institute.[5]

Obesity and Osteoarthritis

Carrying excess weight puts additional pressure on the joints and wears away the soft tissue—cartilage—between joints. This often results in a condition called **osteoarthritis,** a joint swelling and deterioration of the knee, hip, and lower back.

Obesity and Sleep Apnea

Sleep apnea is a serious breathing condition that can affect people who are overweight or obese. This disorder causes a person to snore heavily and, potentially, to stop breathing for short periods during sleep. This sleep interruption often

Special equipment is sometimes needed to help those who suffer from sleep apnea get more restful sleep.

causes daytime sleepiness and, in the most extreme circumstances, can result in heart failure. Doctors say that the risk for sleep apnea increases as body weight increases. Sleep apnea now occurs in about 7 percent of obese children.

Genes, Emotions, and Obesity: The Research Continues

Through research, scientists have come to understand *how* people become obese and overweight. What they do not clearly understand, however, is *why* a person becomes obese.

It seems unlikely, they have concluded, that any person would choose to develop excess fat and its associated health problems, not to mention the social biases society thrusts upon people who are overweight. To answer the "why" question, the American Obesity Association states that obesity is due to three primary factors:

> One of the most intriguing aspects of research into the causes of obesity in recent years is the question of genetics—a person's biological inheritance.

1. genetics (a predisposition to overweight);
2. environmental exposure to an energy-rich food supply and a reduction in physical activity; and
3. personal behavior.[6]

Genetics: Your Biological Inheritance

One of the most intriguing aspects of research into the causes of obesity in recent years is the question of genetics—a person's biological inheritance. Scientists have long known that parents—especially mothers—pass on their

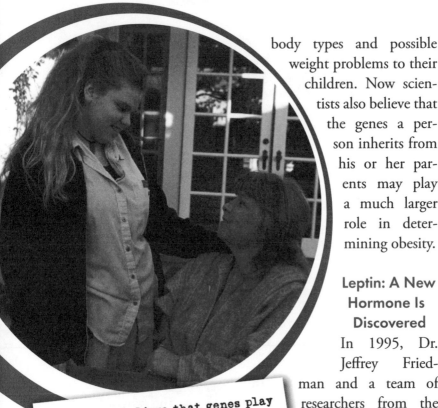

body types and possible weight problems to their children. Now scientists also believe that the genes a person inherits from his or her parents may play a much larger role in determining obesity.

Leptin: A New Hormone Is Discovered

In 1995, Dr. Jeffrey Friedman and a team of researchers from the National Institute of Health discovered a previously unknown hormone they called **leptin.** According to Freidman's research, this hormone is produced by fat tissue in the body and, in normal cases, signals the brain to stop eating when a person is full.

Researchers believe that genes play a large role in determining whether or not a person becomes obese.

A person of normal weight produces more leptin as body fat increases, and this acts as a "brake" on food intake. On the other hand, as body fat decreases in a normal person, the amount of leptin produced decreases. This has the opposite effect on the brain, resulting in a signal to increase food intake. Research by Friedman and other scientists demonstrated that in certain people who

are overweight or obese, a genetic change has caused full or partial loss of leptin.

The Urge for Survival

In addition to this genetic change, Friedman's team identified other hereditary characteristics that control the unconscious urge to eat. The urge for survival is a basic human instinct, and for people who are obese, controlling that urge seems to be biologically impossible. Thus, in an environment of supersized portions and unlimited access to food, these hardwired desires for food result in overconsumption among people who are genetically programmed to become overweight or obese.

"Those who doubt the power of basic drives . . . might note that while one can hold one's breath, this conscious act is soon overcome by the compulsion to breathe," Friedman explained. "[For obese people] the feeling of hunger is . . . probably no less powerful than the drive to drink when one is thirsty."[7]

Many obese people speak of feeling helpless around food. Unfortunately, many people who do not have weight or obesity problems tend to pass judgment on those who do. In general, obese people are criticized. Friedman objects to that criticism:

> "Obesity is not a personal failing. In trying to lose weight, the obese are fighting . . . a battle against biology. While answers are beginning to emerge as to why so many of us are obese, there can be no meaningful discussion on this subject until we resist . . . the belief that with willpower alone, one can . . . resist . . . food and . . . control one's weight."

Unusual Causes of Obesity

In about 1 percent of all cases of people who become obese, weight gain results almost entirely from disease. These diseases include the following:

Hypothyroidism: In this condition, the thyroid gland, which is located in the neck, produces too little of the hormone that controls the body's metabolism. This slowing of the metabolism means that food is not absorbed as quickly as it is in healthy people and results in rapid weight gain.

Cushing's syndrome: This condition results from the excess production of a hormone called cortisol by the adrenal glands, which are located on top of each kidney. This results in a buildup of fat in areas of the body such as the face, upper back, and abdomen.

Other conditions: Obesity can also result from certain inherited conditions and other diseases of the brain.

An adrenal gland is located on top of each kidney.

In addition to these diseases, some medications, such as antidepressants, steroid medications, some high blood pressure drugs, and seizure medications can also result in increased body weight.

Approximately 4 Million Americans Are Binge Eaters

Many people who succumb to the genetic and psychological urges to eat often engage in what is known as binge eating. These are episodes during which overeating is taken to an unhealthy extreme. Binge eaters consume large amounts of food within a period of about 2 hours. They are unable to stop eating even when they are full.

Binge Eaters Represent 2 Percent of the U.S. Population

Psychologists believe that about 2 percent of all adults in the United States—as many as 4 million Americans—are binge eaters. According to the AOA, about 15 percent of people who are overweight have this condition. It is more frequently seen in people who are severely obese. For excessive eating to be classified as a binge eating disorder, the episodes must occur at least twice a week for six months. People who binge eat will:

- eat rapidly;
- eat until feeling uncomfortably full;
- eat when not hungry;
- eat alone because of embarrassment;
- feel disgusted, depressed, or guilty after overeating.

People with a binge eating disorder should get help from a health professional such as a psychiatrist, psychologist, or clinical social worker. Treatment usually focuses on improving self-esteem and confidence rather than on losing weight.

Personal Behavior:
Finding Comfort in Food

While Friedman supports the connection between genes and obesity, the AOA points out a psychological desire to eat that is behavioral rather than genetic. This is the area that the AOA refers to as personal behavior. By this they mean that as people become increasingly overweight, they may experience low self-esteem and, as a result, turn again and again to their only source of comfort: food. For many people who become obese, personal behavior is the starting point for their struggles. According to the AOA, "Many of us learn that food can bring comfort, at least in the short-term. As a result, we often turn to food to heal emotional problems."

Triggers to Eating

Some people who are overweight or obese may face emotional problems such as depression, boredom, loneliness, anxiety, frustration, stress, problems with interpersonal relationships, and poor self-esteem. The AOA recommends that people use psychological tools to identify the situations that trigger their urge to eat. Some of those situations are as follows:

Social. Trying to fit in may cause excessive eating. "Eat something, you'll feel better" is an example of the type of social pressure that may influence the behavior of people who have weight problems.

Overweight teens learn strategies that can help them lose weight.

Isolation. Obese people who are lonely may turn to food as a dependable friend to fill the emptiness in their lives.

Situational. Spurlock pointed out that there were eighty-three McDonald's outlets in Manhattan alone. The modern environment offers many opportunities for overeating at a moment's notice. Situational eating may also occur when people spend most of their time in sedentary activities—sitting around watching TV and movies or playing video games.

Reaching Out for Support

Identifying the situations that trigger the desire to eat—or to overeat—may help people look for alternatives. Some people turn to self-help groups such as Overeaters Anonymous (OA) for support in their effort to control their habit.

In group meetings, overeaters can share feelings with others who have had similar experiences. OA and similar therapy groups may help people avoid the isolation and low self-esteem that often arises as a result of eating problems. In addition to sharing information with fellow overeaters, a group therapy program might also recommend that a person keep a diary of food eaten at each meal, binge episodes, and his or her moods when certain "trigger" situations arise. The opportunity to talk about and to work on attaining individual goals can be life-changing.

Here is one story from a member of OA:

"Many changes have occurred in my life since I graduated from high school. The most significant are the changes that have happened inside me over the six years of my recovery in OA.

In high school I did not eat in the cafeteria with the other students. I ate in a bathroom stall. I now know that compulsive overeaters typically maintain a private relationship with food. I also remember that I was eating because I wanted to stop the embarrassing growling coming from my stomach, not because I was hungry. As the years progressed, I started a pattern of eating after dark. I would slip into some big, comfortable clothing and wait until I was alone.

[When] I went to my 20-year high school reunion this weekend . . . people commented on how shy I used to be. . . . Here I was . . . being extremely outgoing. This is who I am now. . . . I feel beautiful, smart, loving, wise and able to work hard on being me. During the evening, I saw another OAer's face in the crowd. What a gift." [8]

CHAPTER FOUR

Walking Away from Obesity

hen Marcia Potts turned 48 in 2000, she decided to do something about her weight once and for all. Potts was 5 feet, 3 inches (160 cm) tall, and she had been extremely heavy most of her life. There was no mystery about why she was fat, as she explains on the Web site smallstep.gov, which is sponsored by the U.S. Department of Health and Human Services: "I ate all the time and I ate a lot—probably 3,000 to 5,000 calories a day. I could eat a whole large deep-dish pizza by myself. Cheeseburgers were my favorite. Subs. Fries. Lasagna. Things with a lot of cheese. Fattening stuff and lots of it."

Potts had tried many diets throughout the course of her battle with weight, from diet milk shakes to cabbage soup three times a day for weeks. Yet the weight never stayed off, and she began to develop many of the health-related problems associated with obesity, including sleep apnea. This condition became so serious as her weight increased that she was unable to sleep lying down, and the apnea that kept her awake through the night left her so sleep-deprived that she napped at work during the day.

Still, Potts continued to eat. "I ate things 'til they were gone, and they were gone pretty fast. And I never felt full," she says. And she continued to gain more and more weight. "Clothes were a problem," says Potts. "Size 28 was too small. I didn't know where to go to buy clothes."

Potts's health continued to deteriorate. "To walk was unbelievably challenging," she says. "I couldn't breathe. I couldn't stand without leaning or holding onto something. The grocery stores were great because I could hang onto a cart."

Potts became increasingly depressed over her weight. Finally, she called her sister, a nurse, and asked her how she could go about getting a prescription for diet pills. Her sister refused to tell Potts, and instead suggested a weight-loss program that focused on group therapy, keeping a journal, cutting fat and calories, eating smaller portion sizes, and, most importantly, exercising.

On May 23, 2000, Potts joined the program. She remembers the date because as she waited for the bus to take her from her job to the meeting, she had to lean on the mailbox to hold her body up. Then, when she arrived at the location, she weighed in: 317 pounds (144 kg). Her BMI was 56. Her weight was literally killing her.

"I believed I was going to die," she says.

A Commitment to Change: One Meal at a Time

Potts finally made a commitment to change one day—one meal—at a time. In many ways, the formula for losing weight is simple: burn off more calories than you take in. To lose 1 pound (0.45 kg), a person must burn off 3,500 more calories than he or she takes in. Over the course of a week, that means eating about 500 fewer calories a day or burning 500 extra calories a day through exercise. However one does the math—it could be eating 250 fewer calories and burning 250 calories exercising—the result is the same.

How much is 250 calories? There are 250 calories in a normal piece of cake, four cookies, or two sodas. The difference between a meal of a regular cheeseburger (330 calories) and a medium order of french fries (450 calories) instead of a quarter-pound cheeseburger (430 calories) and a large order of french fries (610 calories) is about 260 calories.

Choosing foods that are lower in calories and fat and drinking water instead of sugary drinks are two ways to cut calories.

Potts carefully kept track of everything she drank or ate. She gave up soda and other sweetened beverages. She drank 32 ounces of water every morning—more than half of the four to six glasses of water recommended each day. There were no calories in water, but it made her feel full. Potts lowered her caloric intake to about 1,800 per day. And she made sure that the food she ate was "good" food: filling, nutritious, and fat- and sugar-free.

Ice Cream vs. Fat-Free Yogurt:

You might never choose vanilla fat-free yogurt over a dish of ice cream, but for people like Marcia Potts, this is a choice that can lead to weight loss. Why? Here's a comparison between a serving of ice cream and a serving of fat-free yogurt:

Baskin Robbins Vanilla Ice Cream

Serving size: ½ cup (4 ounces)
Calories: 264
Protein: 4 grams (16 calories)
Fat: 16 grams (144 calories—more than
   60 percent of total)
Carbohydrates: 26 grams (104 calories)

Compare this to the same serving size of fat-free vanilla yogurt:

Fat-Free Vanilla Yogurt

Serving size: ½ cup (4 ounces)
Calories: 130.6
Protein: 6.2 grams (24.8 calories)
Fat: 0.2 grams (1.8 calories)
Carbohydrates: 26 grams
   (104 calories)

Highs and Lows:
The Glycemic Indexes

"I began by going to the salad bar and filling little containers with healthy foods like lettuce, broccoli, mushrooms, and radishes, and ate that."

In changing her diet, Potts began to understand the importance of avoiding foods that are high in sugar and fats.

Nutritionists refer to this diet as a low **glycemic index** diet. The glycemic index refers to changes in blood sugar levels. (As you may recall, glycogen is the scientific term for stored blood sugar.)

Foods with Low Glycemic Index Levels

In recent years, studies have shown that eating foods with low glycemic index levels will keep dieters feeling full and reduce their hunger. Among the foods in this category are oatmeal, peanuts, vegetables, and certain fruits. Lean meats—skinless chicken, for example—and other protein, such as seafood and soy products, also keep glycemic index levels low.

FOR THE RECORD

Soda Is Sweeter Than You Think

Would you eat 14 teaspoons of sugar? If you drink soda, you have! A 12-ounce (355-milliliter) can of soda contains about 14 teaspoons of sugar. Drinking one can of soda per day can cause a weight gain of as much as 15 pounds (6.8 kg) in a year in a person who gets little or no exercise.

Foods with High Glycemic Index Levels

On the other hand, foods with a high glycemic index are generally the foods that Potts and other overweight people most frequently consume. These foods, such as white bread and pasta, contain refined carbohydrates, which cause the glycemic index to rise rapidly. The same holds true for candy, sugary soft drinks, and juices. (See "What's for Breakfast?" in Chapter 2.)

Portion Size

One of the most important points for people who want to lose weight to remember is that portion sizes are almost always much smaller than they think. By thinking of the objects below, people can make sure that their portions are the right size.

3 ounces (85 grams) of meat—the recommended portion for a meal = the size of a deck of cards or a bar of soap

3 ounces (85 grams) of fish = a checkbook

1 ounce (28 grams) cheese = 4 dice

medium potato = a computer mouse

1 cup (56 grams) pasta = a tennis ball

average bagel = a hockey puck

Marcia Potts: Six Weeks and 20 Pounds Lighter

Potts's diet consisted of multiple servings of vegetables per day, and she generally followed an eating plan based on the U.S. government food pyramid. (See page 96). She also made other changes in her diet, such as baking, broiling, or steaming her food rather than frying it. She ate lean red meat—meat without the white marbly fat—and she removed the skin from chicken when she cooked. She also ate more whole-grain foods, which helped her feel full quickly. Potts also paid careful attention to the portion sizes of foods she ate.

Potts spent the first months in the weight-loss program thinking about how and what she ate rather than simply about eating. She got to know what triggered her desire to eat. And, by keeping a diary, she realized that when she got nervous or upset, she looked for food. "I snack," she says. "If I get nervous, I eat. But [now] I eat low-calorie foods."

After six weeks on the diet, Potts had lost 20 pounds

(9 kg). She was surprised because she had failed so often before. But the success she had in just changing what she ate made her more determined. She continued to eat low-calorie foods and to keep a diary of her eating. Instead of setting a distant goal of losing enormous amounts of weight, she made small changes over short periods of time to move toward a goal, such as adding an additional fruit or vegetable into her daily diet.

"In the beginning I had no expectations. I had no idea that I could even get down below 300," she said. "After a while, I didn't crave sweets or greasy foods anymore. It's amazing how your body can adjust."

Potts adjusted so well to the diet that she soon began to lose 20 pounds (9 kg) a month. For the first time, she began to feel encouraged about the possibility of losing weight.

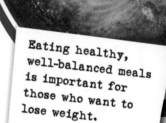

Eating healthy, well-balanced meals is important for those who want to lose weight.

A Determined Marcia Takes a Victory Lap

While changing her diet was an important part of Marcia Potts's fight against obesity, it was only half the battle. The other essential part of losing weight is exercise, which is something she had avoided most of her life. But, determined to change, she began walking almost right away. On her first day in the weight loss program, Potts walked from her apartment to the bus stop from which she traveled to work. It took her about 20 minutes to walk 0.25 mile (0.4 km). Slowly, she began to add a few steps to her daily walk, and she began to walk regularly during her lunch break.

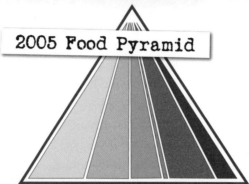

2005 Food Pyramid

Food Groups	Children ages 2 to 6 years, women, some older adults (about 1,600 calories)	Older children, teen girls, active women, most men (about 2,200 calories)	Teen boys, active men (about 2,800 calories)
Breads, Cereal, Rice, and Pasta Group (Grains Group)- especially whole grain	6	9	11
Vegetable Group	3	4	5
Fruit Group	2	3	4
Milk, Yogurt, and Cheese Group (Milk Group)- preferably fat free or low fat	2 or 3*	2 or 3*	2 or 3*
Meat, Poultry, Fish, Dry Beans, Eggs and Nuts Group (Meat and Beans Group)- preferably lean or low fat	2, for a total of 5 ounces	2, for a total of 6 ounces	3, for a total of 7 ounces

Adapted from U.S. Department of Agriculture, Center for Nutrition Policy and Promotion. The Food Guide Pyramid, Home and Garden Bulletin Number 252, 1996.

*The number of servings depends on your age. Older children and teenagers (ages 9 to 18 years) and adults over the age of 50 need 3 servings daily. Others need 2 servings daily. During pregnancy and lactation, the recommended number of Milk Group servings is the same as for nonpregnant women.

In July, only two months after beginning the program, Potts decided to try swimming in the outdoor pool at her apartment building. "On July 13, I swam my first lap," she says. By then, she had lost nearly 40 pounds (18 kg).

FACTS & STATS

The CDC's Recommended Daily Amount of Exercise

The chart below shows a wide range of physical activities and the amount of time one would have to perform the activity to burn the recommended daily minimum of 150 calories. They range from more to less vigorous. The less vigorous an activity is, the longer it has to be done to burn enough recommended daily calories.

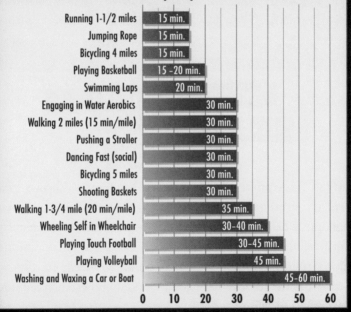

Number of Minutes of Activity Required to Burn 150 kcalories

Activity	Minutes
Running 1-1/2 miles	15 min.
Jumping Rope	15 min.
Bicycling 4 miles	15 min.
Playing Basketball	15 - 20 min.
Swimming Laps	20 min.
Engaging in Water Aerobics	30 min.
Walking 2 miles (15 min/mile)	30 min.
Pushing a Stroller	30 min.
Dancing Fast (social)	30 min.
Bicycling 5 miles	30 min.
Shooting Baskets	30 min.
Walking 1-3/4 mile (20 min/mile)	35 min.
Wheeling Self in Wheelchair	30-40 min.
Playing Touch Football	30-45 min.
Playing Volleyball	45 min.
Washing and Waxing a Car or Boat	45-60 min.

Source: Centers for Disease Control and Prevention, "Physical Activity for Everyone: Recommendations: How Active Do Adults Need to Be to Gain Some Benefit?", http://www.cdc.gov/nccdphp/dnpa/physical/recommendations/adults.htm.

Exercise is an important part of a weight loss program.

Exercise: Guidelines from the Surgeon General

Health researchers and doctors have long known that regular exercise is beneficial for people of all ages. But for people who are overweight or obese, exercise can make a critical difference between success and failure in weight-loss attempts. How much exercise do we need? In 2004, a report issued by the U.S. Surgeon General established new exercise guidelines:

- For relatively fit adults with a BMI in the normal range, the Surgeon General's office recommends 30 minutes of moderate exercise per day.

- For people whose BMI places them in the overweight category and who are trying to lose weight, the Surgeon General's office recommends as much as 60 minutes of moderate daily exercise.

Moderate vs. Vigorous Exercise

Russell Pate, a University of South Carolina professor who served on the advisory committee that established the exercise guidelines, said that it was difficult to determine exactly how much exercise an overweight person needs. The differences in a person's daily caloric intake and his or her basal metabolic rate plays a role in the amount of exercise needed to lose weight. Pate's research showed that many overweight people who exercised 30 minutes a day did not lose weight. It was for that reason, Pate explained, that the surgeon general's final report recommends up to 60 minutes per day of moderate exercise for people attempting to lose weight.

"If you are meeting the 30-minutes-a-day recommendation and not losing weight, you should increase your amount of exercise," said Pate.[1] For many people who strive to lose weight, the term *moderate physical exercise* is unclear. Examples of moderate intensity include walking at between 3 and 4 miles per hour (4.8 and 6.4 km per hour) or applying similar exertion to cycling, swimming, or other activities. The next category of exercise, vigorous, includes cycling, running, swimming, full-court basketball, or cross-country skiing.

People who exercise vigorously burn calories faster than people who engage in moderate exercise. Thus, they can reach their recommended daily exercise goal more quickly than those who engage in longer, less-intense workouts. For example, a person who runs a mile in 7 minutes burns the same amount of calories as a person who walks a mile in 20 minutes or jogs the mile in 10. In other words, a vigorous 20-minute workout equals a moderate 30-minute workout.

In terms of overall calories burned, a general rule is that moderate exercise should burn between 4 and 7 calories per minute. That means that a moderate 30-minute workout should ideally burn between 150 and 200 calories. Over the course of a week, that comes out to about 1,000 calories burned.

Some doctors recommend 60 minutes a day of moderate activity for people who are trying to lose weight.

Do You Have the Right Balance?

OUTPUT
Calories Used During Physical Activity

INTAKE
Calories from Foods

THE ENERGY BALANCE

Source: Department of Health and Human Services, 2004.

The Department of Health and Human Services developed the image above to show that the key to maintaining a healthy weight is balancing the amount of calories taken in with the amount expended. Here are some points that people who want to lose weight might consider:

- One small chocolate-chip cookie—about 50 calories—equals a brisk 10-minute walk.
- The difference between a large gourmet chocolate-chip cookie and a small chocolate chip cookie is equal to about 40 minutes of raking leaves, which will burn about 200 calories.
- One hour of walking at a moderate pace—about 20 minutes per mile—burns about the same amount of energy contained in one jelly doughnut, about 300 calories.
- In order to balance the intake from a fast-food meal of a double cheeseburger, large fries, and a 24-ounce soft drink, a person would have to run 2.5 hours at a 10 minutes/mile pace—that would burn 1,500 calories.

Exercise Speeds Metabolism

The good news for people like Potts, who are dedicated to losing weight, is that consistent exercise helps to speed up the metabolism. In others words, as a person exercises regularly, he or she becomes fitter. And the more physically fit a person is, the faster he or she loses fat.

> Depending on how vigorous a physical activity is, says the CDC, one's body may burn calories for as long as two hours after finishing exercise.

The reason for this is simple: muscle tissue has a higher metabolic rate than adipose tissue. So it's logical that replacing fat with muscle through exercise will create a snowball effect, as increased amounts of exercise lead to more efficient burning of calories. Depending on how vigorous a physical activity is, says the CDC, one's body may burn calories for as long as two hours after finishing exercise.

Marcia Potts: Five Years and Almost 200 Pounds Lighter

Potts's case illustrates how exercise becomes increasingly beneficial. At first, walking slowly for twenty minutes was as much as she could manage. Yet within two months, she was able to begin swimming, and she had added ten minutes to her daily exercise routine. By that point, she was losing 20 pounds (9 kg) per month. In early 2001, seven months into her weight-loss program, she joined a deepwater running class at a local workout facility. "There I met an instructor, Sally Dimsdale, who became very important to me. She challenged me," says Potts.

Potts continued to lose weight. As her fitness level increased, with her instructor's approval, she joined classes in water aerobics and weight training. This combination of aerobic exercise—building her lung and heart efficiency—with strength training caused the pounds to drop away at an increasingly rapid rate. After one year, Potts had lost 163 pounds (74 kg).

Today, five years after she was morbidly obese, Potts weighs 129 pounds (59 kg)—a weight loss of slightly under 200 pounds

Water aerobics provides a good cardiovascular workout and is easy on knees and other joints.

(91 kg). Her BMI has dropped from 56 to 23. Many of her old work colleagues don't recognize the woman whose weight was once killing her. "They probably think I died," she says.

The Upside to Lifting Weights

Potts's program—especially adding weight training—is highly recommended by many exercise specialists. It's not necessary to become a bodybuilder, health experts say. Simply using light weights to firm and tone muscle tissue is beneficial.

Health professionals also recommend training for adolescents who are overweight or obese. In many cases, heavy kids are among the strongest in their peer group, and lifting weights can help them build energy-burning muscle tissue to replace adipose tissue.

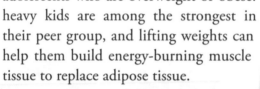

Weight training helps replace fat tissue with muscle tissue.

While some kids might lift weights at home, the availability of exercise equipment and time to work out has brought attention once again to the role of schools in helping kids battle obesity. In this case, the focus has turned to physical education and the lack of programs for adolescents. According to the CDC, only 28 percent of high-school students nationwide attended a daily physical education class in 2003. During the same year, according to the CDC, 38 percent of high school students watched television for 3 hours or more each school night.

Who's Going to Gym Class? Who Isn't?

According to the CDC, the percentage of kids who exercised in school dropped as they became older. Thus, while 71 percent of freshmen were in gym class at least one day a week in 2003, only 40 percent of the seniors attended gym daily. In either case, according to experts, one day of exercise per week is not enough for any student, regardless of his or her weight.

The CDC research also found that student participation in physical education varied from state to state. In Tennessee, for example, only 18 percent of seniors participated in a physical-education class. In New York, however, more than 90 percent of seniors had gym class at least

Fast-Food Fitness
with Ronald Mcdonald

In addition to offering healthier meal choices, in January 2005, McDonald's Corporation began to address the issue of exercise. McDonald's began to offer meals with salads and a pedometer to measure distance walked or run every day. The company also reached out to children by sending its red-haired "spokesclown," Ronald McDonald, into elementary schools to talk about fitness.

Athletes Carl Lewis and Jackie Joyner-Kersee share a laugh in front of a McDonald's banner. McDonald's was one of the sponsors of the 2004 Olympic Games.

Ronald McDonald as Health Ambassador

In a news release, the company called Ronald McDonald its "ambassador for an active, balanced lifestyle." Research shows that Ronald McDonald is one of the most widely recognized figures among young children. He has visited schools to teach about such issues as bike safety and literacy. Now, according to the company spokesperson, "Ronald does not promote food, but fun and activity."[2]

Plan Draws Criticism and Praise

Not everyone praised the company for its plan. Psychologist Susan Linn, author of *Consuming Kids*, said that Ronald McDonald "has no place in the school. The amount of exercise it will take to exercise off everything these kids consume will take all day." [3]

The American Academy of Pediatrics, however, felt that any attempt to fight obesity in its earliest stages was worthwhile. Reginald L. Washington, co-chairman of the academy's task force on obesity, said the program was a good way to "take advantage of the fact that Ronald McDonald has such recognition with kids that if he tells them to get moving, maybe they will do it."

once a week. In grades below high school, figures were similar. The National Association for Sport and Physical Education reports that Illinois is the only state that requires daily physical education K–12, while Alabama requires it for K–8.

Feeling Restless? You're Burning Calories!

According to research from the Mayo Clinic in Rochester, Minnesota, normal or thin people spend an average of two hours a day on their feet, pacing, tapping their feet, and moving restlessly.[4]

Do such small movements matter? "Yes," said Dr. James Levine, the endocrinologist and nutritionist at the Mayo Clinic, who directed the study. People who fidget burn about 350 calories a day—more than twice as many calories as are recommended by the CDC's minimal exercise standards. In well-balanced circumstances, this alone could result in a loss of 30 to 40 pounds (14 to 18 kg) in one year without a single trip to the gym.

Small changes, such as taking the stairs instead of an elevator, can help increase weight loss.

For his study, Levine recruited twenty volunteers—ten lean men and women and ten slightly obese people. No matter what their weight, none of the volunteers engaged in regular exercise. All called themselves couch potatoes.

A NEAT Study

Levine's team attached sensors to special underwear that measured body movements every half-second for ten-day periods over several months. During the ten-day periods, they had to wear the underwear around the clock, taking it off only to shower and to get a fresh set from the researchers. What they wanted to measure was what they called **NEAT**, or non-exercise activity thermogenesis. These are the calories people burn during everyday activities such as sitting, walking, pacing, or just standing.

25 Million Pieces of Data Collected!

By the end of the study, researchers had collected 25 million pieces of data on each participant. The data revealed that the obese people in the study were more apt to remain sedentary. In other words, they had a lower NEAT rate than the lean subjects. Levine's research also determined that the difference in activity levels may have resulted from a difference in levels of certain brain chemicals that control a person's urge to move. Just as an imbalance in the hormone leptin (see Chapter 3) makes obese people continue to eat after they are full, a different brain chemical imbalance creates a tendency to be inactive.

NEAT Is within the Reach of Everyone

By making small changes in their daily behavior—such as walking up stairs rather than taking an elevator—people can burn off calories without even thinking about it. In fact, Levine explained, a person burns 10 percent more calories simply standing instead of sitting. And walking 1 mile an hour faster can increase calorie burn by 100 percent.

"These actions are entirely doable, because [they] do not require special or large spaces, unusual training regimens, or gear," Levine added. "Unlike running a marathon, NEAT is within the reach of everyone."[5]

FOR THE RECORD

Someone You Know Is a Couch Potato
Is it you? The President's Council on Physical Fitness and Sports estimates that only one in five Americans exercises for a minimum of twenty minutes, three or more days a week. The average American gets less than fifty minutes of exercise per week. Three out of five Americans do not exercise.

Conclusion

Even before articles about Levine's study appeared in the national news media in early 2005, his recommendations for non-exercise activity were being publicized by U.S. government Web sites, including a site sponsored by the Department of Health and Human Services, www.smallstep. gov. The tips at Small Step include simple physical and dietary advice to help Americans lose weight. Suggestions for easily done activities include mowing the lawn with a push mower, sitting up straight at work, taking the wheels off suitcases, and taking the stairs instead of the escalator.

Small Step is the same site that tells the story of Marcia Potts. Although she may have started with rather small steps, she made certain that she kept going. Says fitness trainer Sally Dimsdale, "Marcia is one of the most disciplined people I know. No excuses. She was single-minded. She truly believed every step she took, every stair she took,

and every bite of food—the right kind of food—brought her closer to her goal. She was so motivated."

Obesity has become one of the most critical health issues facing the United States today. This book has explored many of the factors at play in what many people call the obesity crisis: from Monster Thickburgers to couch potatoes. Whether you or someone you know struggles with weight, perhaps this book will suggest ways that all Americans can work together to address the issue of obesity in the United States. In the end, it is a responsibility shared by all who believe that a healthy nation is a worthwhile goal.

Former Surgeon General David Satcher puts it this way in his report "Call to Action":

> "Many people believe that dealing with overweight and obesity is a personal responsibility. To some degree they are right, but it is also a community responsibility. When there are no safe, accessible places for children to play or adults to walk, jog, or ride a bike, that is a community responsibility. When school lunchrooms or office cafeterias do not provide healthy and appealing food choices, that is a community responsibility."[6]

Glossary

Adipose tissue: Body tissue that is composed of adipocytes, or fat cells

Agoraphobia: A fear of open spaces

Amino acids: Molecules that make up protein

Atherosclerosis: A disease that occurs when blood vessels—arteries, veins, and capillaries—are narrowed by cholesterol buildup

Basal metabolic rate (BMR): The rate at which the body uses energy to keep the heart beating, the lungs breathing, the kidneys functioning, and the body temperature steady

Blood Pressure: A measure of the amount of force required to pump blood to and from the heart

Body mass index (BMI): A number, usually between 18 and 25, that determines whether a person is underweight, normal, overweight, or obese, calculated by dividing one's weight in pounds by height in inches squared and multiplying by 703

Calorie: The amount of energy, or heat, it takes to raise the temperature of 1 gram of water 1 degree Celsius (1.8 degrees Fahrenheit)

Carbohydrates: The basic components of food that provide the body with energy.

Cholesterol: A waxy, fatlike compound found in foods, in the bloodstream, and in the body's cells, which is critical for protecting cell membranes but can obstruct arteries

Diabetes: A disease that results from an imbalance between the amount of glucose in the blood and the presence of a hormone called insulin

Fat: A basic component of food that stores energy in the body

Gallbladder: A small, saclike organ located on the right side of the abdomen beneath the liver

Gallstones: Hard particles of cholesterol that form when foods high in carbohydrates, fats, and sugar flood the liver with an oversupply of cholesterol

Glucose: A simple sugar produced in plants and animals by the conversion of carbohydrates, proteins, and fats

Glycogen: the scientific term for blood sugar

Glycemic index: a measurement of the amount of glycogen contained in foods

Hypothalamus: A central area in the brain that controls involuntary functions like body temperature, hunger, and the release of hormones

Heart: A hollow muscular organ that pumps blood through the body and controls circulation

Insulin: A hormone secreted by the pancreas that enables cells to absorb glucose, fatty acids, and amino acids

Kidneys: Two bean-shaped organs located in the middle of the back that remove wastes from the bloodstream

Leptin: A recently discovered hormone that is produced by fatty tissue in the body and signals the brain to stop eating when a person is full

Liver: An organ that produces a chemical called bile, which helps to break down fats for absorption in the blood

Metabolic syndrome: A combination of health risks that develop over a period of time and exist simultaneously, including high blood pressure, poor blood-sugar control, and high levels of fats in the blood

Metabolism: The process by which food is broken down into molecules in the digestive tract and sent through the bloodstream to the cells

NEAT: Non-exercise activity thermogenesis, a measure of the calories people burn during everyday activities such as sitting, walking, pacing, or just standing

Osteoarthritis: A disease process in which the bones and cartilage of the body's joints break down

Overweight: Having a BMI between 25 and 30

Obese: Having a BMI of 30 and above

Panniculus: Excess adipose tissue that hangs downward from the waist below the abdomen

Pancreas: The organ in the body that produces glucagon and insulin

Thermic effect: The effect produced by the body's need for energy in order to digest food

Source Notes

Introduction

1. MSNBC staff, "Hardee's serves up 1,420-calorie burger," news release, November 17, 2004, http://www.msnbc.mcn.com/id/6498304/.
2. Centers for Disease Control and Prevention (CDC), "Prevalence of Overweight and Obesity among Adults: United States, 1999–2002," http://www.cdc.gov/nchs/products/pubs/pubd/hestats/obese/obse99.htm.
3. Ibid.
4. Mita Sanghavi Goel, Ellen P. McCarthy, Russell S. Phillips, and Christina C. Wee, "Obesity Among U.S. Immigrant Subgroups by Duration of Residence," *JAMA,* 2004, 292: 2860–2867.
5. American Public Health Association (2003), http://www.apha.org/legislative/policy/2003/2003-017.pdf.

Chapter One

1. Ali H. Mokdad, James S. Marks, Donna F. Stroup, Julie L. Gerberding, "Actual Causes of Death in the United States, 2000,"*JAMA,* 2004, 291: 1238–1245.

2. Testimony before the Subcommittee on Education Reform Committee on Education and the Workforce, United States House of Representatives, July 16, 2003, "The Obesity Crisis in America," statement of Richard H. Carmona, Surgeon General U.S. Public Health Service, Acting Assistant Secretary for Health, Department of Health and Human Services.

3. National Health and Nutrition Examination Survey, http://www.cdc.gov/nhanes/pQuestions.htm#Participants.

4. W. Stewart Agras, "Children of Obese Parents Face Highest Risk of Being Overweight," http://mednews.stanford.edu/releases/2004/july/obesity.html.

5. American Obesity Association, "My Story," #9, http://www.obesity.org/subs/story/entirestory.shtml.

6. Institute of Medicine, "Preventing Childhood Obesity: Health in the Balance," September 30, 2004, http://www.iom.edu/report.asp?id=22596.

7. Tracy Jan, "N.H. weighs students to monitor for obesity," *The Boston Globe,* December 30, 2004, http://www.boston.com/news/local/articles/2004/12/30/nh_weighs_students_to_monitor_for_obesity/.

8. Ibid.

9. American Obesity Association, http://www.obesity.org/.

Chapter 2

1. "Obesity rising sharply among U.S. preschoolers," January 30, 2004, http://www.cnn.com/2004/HEALTH/conditions/12/30/childhood.obesity/.

2. Linda Bren, "Losing Weight: Start by Counting Calories," originally published January–February 2002 issue of *FDA Consumer,* revised April 2004.

Chapter 3

1. Sharon Waxman, "Reporter's Notebook: From Imelda Marcos's Flats to the Golden Arches," *New York Times,* January 30, 2004.
2. Steven Dabkowski, "Spitting chips, McDonald's fights back." *The Age,* June 14, 2004.
3. AICR press release, "New Scientific Thinking Implicates Body Fat as Cancer Promoter, Excess Fat May Act as Continuous 'Hormone Pump'," *Raising Risk,* July 11, 2002.
4. Ibid.
5. Rob Stein, "New Diagnosis for Overweight," *Washington Post,* February 8, 2005, p. A01.
6. Morgan Downey, "It's Your Fault," American Obesity Association, February 7, 2002, http://www.obesity.org/subs/editorial/fault.shtml.
7. Rockefeller University press release, "Obesity not a personal failing, says leptin discoverer Jeffrey Friedman, but a battle against biology," Rockefeller University, February 6, 2003, http://www.rockefeller.edu/pubinfo/020603.php.
8. Overeaters Anonymous, "How OA Changed My Life," http://oa.org.yourmis.com/how_oa_changed.html.

Chapter 4

1. Sally Squires, "Revised Diet Guidelines Urge Exercise," *Washington Post,* January 13, 2005, p. A01.
2. Caroline Mayer, McDonald's Makes Ronald a Health Ambassador," *Washington Post,* January 28, 2005, p. E01.

3. Ibid.

4. Rob Stein, "Fidgeting Helps Separate the Lean From the Obese, Study Finds," *Washington Post,* January 28, 2005.

5. Eric Ravussin, "Physiology: A NEAT Way to Control Weight?," *Science,* 2005, 307: 530–531.

6. U.S. Department of Health and Human Services news release, "Overweight and Obesity Threaten U.S. Health Gains," December 13, 2001.

To Find Out More

Books

Critser, Greg. *Fat Land: How Americans Became the Fattest People in the World.* Boston: Mariner Books, 2004.

Gordon, Melanie Apel. *Let's Talk about Being Overweight.* New York: Powerkids Press, 2001.

Lynch, Chris. *Extreme Elvin.* New York: Harper Trophy, 2001.

Schlosser, Eric. *Fast Food Nation.* Boston: Houghton Mifflin, 2001.

Shell, Ellen. *The Hungry Gene: The Science of Fat and the Future of Thin.* Boston: Atlantic Monthly Press, 2002.

Summerfield, Liane. *Nutrition, Exercise, and Behavior: An Integrated Approach to Weight Management.* Stamford, CT: Brooks Cole, 2000.

Turck, Mary. *Healthy Snack & Fast-Food Choices.* Minneapolis: LifeMatters Press, 2001.

DVD/Film

Super Size Me: A Film of Epic Proportions. Produced and directed by Morgan Spurlock. Samuel Goldwyn Films, 2004.

Web Sites

American Obesity Association
http://www.obesity.org/

Centers for Disease Control and Prevention
http://www.cdc.gov/

KidsHealth
http://www.kidshealth.org/kid/misc/about.html

Index

About the Author

Scott Ingram is the author of more than 40 books for young people. He lives in Portland, Connecticut. A former teacher and magazine editor, he keeps his BMI in the normal range with long rides on his bicycle whenever the weather cooperates.